"I have observed that verbal or physical abuse is destructive to all involved. Unless the cycle is broken, this behavior will continue. God helped Kathy to break the cycle."

—Esther McChesney,
Probation officer/supervisor,
Snohomish County Juvenile Court

"As a fellow survivor, Kathy's book has helped lead me down a new path in my life towards healing. Her beautiful soul shines through her work."

—Lindsey Johnson,
An abuse survivor

"Kathy stepped forward with great courage to write about a subject that is so often kept in the background. Kathy exposes this abuse for what it is...SIN."

—Carolyn Findlay Davis,
Retired RN, former educator,
Published author

A Vision Beyond Abuse

Spiritual Healing After Abuse

Kathy Goodhew

A Vision Beyond Abuse

Spiritual Healing After Abuse

Copyright © 2010, 2017 by Kathy Goodhew.

All rights reserved.

Kathy Goodhew previously published original edition under following copyright.
A Vision Beyond Abuse © 2010 Kathy Goodhew. All rights reserved.
Library of Congress Catalog Number TX 7-814-141

No part of this publication may be reproduced by any means without the written permission of the author.

Scriptures taken from World English Bible (WEB)

Manufactured in the United States of America

Vision Beyond Abuse

Spiritual healing after abuse

Written by
Kathy Goodhew

www.kathygoodhew.com

Book design copyright © 2017 by Kathy Goodhew, All rights reserved
Cover and interior design by Kathy Goodhew

ISBN-13: 978-1544894645

DEDICATION

**In memory of my brother, David, he inspired me
to take the next step on my path.**

ACKNOWLEDGMENTS

The Triune God; for his grace he gave
by walking with me through the darkness.

My husband Michael; for his skill
of knowing when I needed to talk.

My mother Betty; for she, along with Dad,
led me on this trek of faith.

My sister Mary; for walking with me down
memory lane as we worked on edits.

Rev. Doctor Robert Higgins guidance
as he taught me about the true nature of Jesus Christ.

Pastor John Mason and his spirit-filled words,
"Jesus what are you doing here and how can I be a part of it,"
triggering me to publish my story about abuse.

CONTENTS

Foreword	11
Introduction	13
Dreams	21
Imitation of Love	25
Seeing the Truth	33
A New Storm Descends	38
This Is My Season	44
'Wounded' Poetry Collection	49
Afterword	55
About the Author	58

FOREWORD

DOMESTIC VIOLENCE AND THE DEMEANING OF WOMEN in all its ugly forms is rampant in our culture. This book tells the story of one woman's survival and escape as Kathy is transformed from being a victim to becoming a wounded healer. This must-read book exposes the external and internal destructiveness of violence that no woman should ever accept as inevitable or normal! The unseen, intimate companion came alongside Kathy as guide and friend in a way to reveal God's power to heal and bring forth new and greater life.

"We know that all things work together for good for those who love God, to those who are called according to his purpose." (Romans 8:28). World English Bible (WEB)

—Rev. Dr. Robert C. Higgins, Kathy's
pastor and friend for forty years

INTRODUCTION

Have you ever had a dream that persistently haunted you over a lengthy period? I did. Long after the demise of two disastrous relationships, I chose to ignore the pain that I endured within those relationships. This pain was the consequence of suffering emotional, verbal, psychological, and physical abuse.

Even though I managed to walk away from both relationships, I continued to deny that abuse left me emotionally scarred. My emotional baggage tagged along with me for a long ride. Nevertheless, the bones of my broken past refused to release me from their hold. Perhaps that is why my haunting dreams materialized. These dreams plagued me for three decades, even though I genuinely wanted to be free of them and the past. However, I did not know how to accomplish this goal. My dreams were persistent and sometimes an added terror would visit, leaving me shaking and blanketed with cold sweats.

The thirty-year dream anniversary had arrived about the time of the unexpected death of my brother, triggering something like a stirring in the air. I believe that the stirring was bringing change and that stirring was inside of me. I was broken, but God had a plan as He stirred and stirred in order to heal my wounds. I believe that in that critical moment, an all-knowing God heard my humble prayer; *may this place be where I can surrender my grief so my soul might be soothed by God's Holy and compassionate love.*

"For I know the thoughts that I think toward you, says Yahweh, thoughts of peace, and not of evil, to give you hope in your latter end" (Jeremiah 29:11) World English Bible (WEB)

My story is about finding healing, not about placing blame on anyone that mistreated or victimized me, because we are all flawed. Even with all of our flaws, we can still bring glory to God. It is my understanding that we are all a work-in-progress.

A good example of flawed people is King David from the Bible in the Old Testament. David wanted to serve God as a boy and even later while in power. While a boy, King Saul liked David very much, because he was able to soothe the King with music. David's success grew after slaying the Philistine giant. We can also remember that along with being a musician, David was a talented composer. However, he was a man troubled with character flaws. He may have been strong in in the battlefield, but was weak at home. He may have been a man of success, but suffered failure in his supremacy. He may have been a champion, but later in life he had many difficulties. Even so, David continued to serve God. The Bible reminds us that he was a man after God's heart.

Therefore, there is hope for everyone. We can all receive redemption. Therefore, I do not judge when I know the Son of God will come and rightly judge all of humanity.

Whether we admit it or not each of us has the capacity of dark and light within us. The dark breathes dislike, jealousy, untruths, bitterness, or even self-disgust. The light breathes harmony, compassion, courage, humbleness, and honesty. Every day we face a battle of wills and God will not relent until we release our will to Him.

"For we must all be revealed before the judgment seat of Christ; that each one may receive the things in the body, according to what he has done, whether good or bad." (2 Corinthians 5:10)

My role here is that of a wounded healer, sharing my personal struggle with a word of caution and a promise of hope. For a long time I was silent about my broken past, because as I previously said, I just wanted to forget about the abuse and try to move on. Therefore, I know first-hand how a victim might feel. I am sharing my perspective about a complex issue as a way to help everyone better understand what it is to be a victim of abuse. It is not about love. It is not about attractiveness. It is about power. It is about control. It lets you know that you have given up your human rights. It reveals that your limit of what is unacceptable does not matter. It is called ABUSE.

Living in a state of fear can negatively affect your health. It may even consume a person if there is no action taken. If a person does not stand up for their human rights then the offender wins. If we want to thrive, we must find the eye in the storm where there is calm so we can find our inner strength.

Many abuse survivors carry around long-term, hidden scars. Ask any abuse survivor this question. *Have you ever been afraid to go home to the one you love?* Pay close attention. You just might see a hint of fear lurking in the victims' eyes while denying that anything is wrong, which is a sign that something is off. Temperament and behavior changes might be the most obvious sign, while other signs may be more subtle. The victim may appear overly anxious or walk on eggshells whenever their partner is around. The victim might begin to wear sunglasses or clothing unsuitable for the season so they can conceal bruising. They may even create excuses for their partner's behavior. Consequently, many abuse victims will climb into an invisible shell and conceal their heartbreak, loneliness, and despair so they can survive their own personal battlefield. Yet, what many victims do not realize is that God offers everyone abundant strength. It lies within every victim waiting to emerge to protect his or her children or themselves.

Abuse comes in different forms. It comes as neglect, verbal abuse, physical abuse, emotional abuse, psychological abuse, hate crimes, and sexual abuse. Sexual abuse entails any form of exploitation, manipulation, and submission to attain deviant sensual gratification. All forms of abuse carry the same intent; crushing the spirit of another human being. There is a power struggle going on within every abusive relationship and it begins when one person controls by holding power over the other person for his or her own gratification.

When people think of domestic abuse, they often picture those who have physically assaulted women. However, not all abusive relationships involve violence. Just because you are not visibly battered and bruised does not mean you are not a victim of abuse. Many men and women suffer from emotional abuse, which is no less destructive and life altering. Unfortunately, emotional abuse often goes unnoticed or minimized.

As a past victim, I am inclined to include my own assessment about the challenges for victims of abuse. Domestic abuse will continue until we acknowledge its destructive nature. Many victims happen to be women, but that does not mean that men are not vulnerable, because they too can become a victim. The victim often times feels powerless and is hesitant to speak up out of fear of retaliation by the abuser. Meanwhile, the rest of the communities consider abuse as an invisible nuisance and ignore the long-standing consequences for anyone struggling to survive in an abusive relationship. Consequently, abuse and all of its ugliness is on the rise with long-lasting after-effects linked to domestic abuse. If left the way it is, domestic abuse becomes more violent and will continue to be the leading cause of injury or death to abuse victims in the United States.

Therefore, if you find that someone is ridiculing, taunting, rebuking you, or causing a feeling of doubt and low self-esteem, you are not alone. Be brave, and do not allow anyone to tell you that you are unfit or useless. This is just a tactic used to gain control over you. Instead, know that in God's eyes, you are precious and lovable.

The good news in the midst of this data is that there are survivors of abuse! The survivors are those who have been able to walk away and break their silence by telling someone. By getting help, they have been able to break the destructive cycle, hoping for change.

I must not forget the abuser. The abuser is not a fiendish monster though sometimes the victim might think of the abuser as such in the midst of an assault. An abuser is simply a human being with far-reaching flaws that are untreated. Some abusers struggle greatly to break free from their power compulsion, yet others would rather live in denial. I am not an expert, but there are various reasons why people may abuse others. I have included my own perspective about why someone might become an abuser.

1) Some abusers may have learned to abuse because they themselves suffered abuse by a parent or by someone else that they saw as an authority figure. Subsequently, they felt powerless and saw the abuse as a normal state. Over time, they may reach their limit and refuse to be victim by becoming the abuser to gain power again.
2) Mental health and addiction might be a reason, trouble managing their anger, explosive disorders, drinking or drugs.
3) Compassion deficit may play a role, due to a brain injury or because somehow, their ability to show compassion never developed properly, creating indifference.

Why doesn't the victim just leave? Since I have first-hand knowledge, I can say that this is an insensitive question to ask any survivor of abuse. Still, many people have thoughtlessly asked me the question. Perhaps a healthier approach might be this question, **why do abusers feel the need to threaten and hurt the one they supposedly love.** I am sure there are multiple reasons for both questions. I do know from my own broken past that there are abuse survivors who have broken the abuse cycle by leaving their abuser. On the other hand, a major reason why a victim might be reluctant to leave is that they sense that they will be in greater danger if the abuser thinks that he or she might lose power thus triggering desperation, and desperation fuels harsher assaults when leave-taking seems imminent.

Lastly, no matter the situation, life carries on. Because of this, one can move forward or stay paralyzed in the past. With God's guidance, I chose to move forward by facing my pain. My story shows the effects of living in an abusive relationship that is dysfunctional and a poor imitation of love. It also reveals my challenge in the wilderness of despair.

The Exodus story reminds us how the Israelites grumbled to Moses and tested God while roaming the desert wilderness. I too lived in the wilderness. I did not know it at the time; it was God's way for me to find a deeper understanding of Him. God was slowly leading me on a path of surrender so I might begin to trust and give my heart to Him fully.

I had to dig deep inside for buried memories for clarity. When I learned to place my trust in Jesus, He began to push away the fog and provided answers. Much like a tapestry, He steered me to weave specific life moments with my budding faith in Him.

Writing it all down led me into a time of great distress. With each word penned, my insides churned and my eyes teared, but I gradually began to see things in a fresh way. Writing was a healing balm and I began to grasp the revealing significance of the recurring dreams. My broken parts were starting to heal as I felt God's peace flow over me. I envisioned myself in His garden of healing. If you believe God's promise, you can also find His garden of healing after abuse.

"He heals the broken in heart, and binds up their wounds." (Psalm 147:3) World English Bible (WEB)

Cycle of Abuse

1. Tension builds, interaction breaks down, and victim reacts by pacifying the abuser.

2. An incident occurs via verbal, anger, arguing, blaming, intimidation, coercion, psychological, or physical abuse.

3. Reconciliation attempt with apologies, excuses, abuser minimizes the abuse or even denies it happened, blames the victim.

4. Calmness washes over the abuser. Abuser forgets the incident and thinks that all is well and a loving couple again.

Those Targeted By Abuse

Children

Elderly Women

Men

College Students

Workers

Anyone Different

What to Do If Abused

- Recognize that it is abuse

- Talk to someone
    - Family member
    - Friend
    - Pastor
    - Doctor
    - Counsellor
    - Fireman or Police

- Decide to leave or stay
    - Consider if the situation can improve
    - Decide how long to give the abuser to make an effort to change. If staying, set limits of acceptable behavior and protect yourself.
- Know what to do in case of emergency
    - Know ahead where you can go and how you will get there.
    - Find someone to take care of your pets.

- Make an emergency plan
    - Establish an escape route
    - Make copies of your identification
    - Keep an emergency bag with essentials and money at a friend's house

- Make a list (in safe place) of HELP phone numbers
    - Crisis phone
    - Emergency 911 number

Abuse Checklist

- Does someone monitor your movements?

- Does abuser stop you from seeing friends or family?

- Does abuser belittle you?"

- Are you afraid to disagree or say NO?

- Does abuser accuse you of flirting with others when it is not true?

- Does abuser control the money or not let you have money?

- Does abuser stop you from seeking medical help?

- Does abuser threaten or hurt you in a violent manner?

- Does abuser pledge no harm the next time?

- Have you been forced to engage in sensual activity against your will?

DREAMS

I have been able to recall dreams my entire life, especially the more dramatic ones. I have had good ones and bad ones. Anyhow, it never occurred to me that I owned a unique gift given to me by God. The Triune God blessed me with the gift of remembering and later, making sense of dreams. With God at the helm, he provided my dreams to guide me during the course of my life. God has shown me repeatedly within my dreams and during my wakefulness of His constant faithfulness and I feel blessed.

Some of my dreams were a one-time occurrence. Once, I dreamed that a large grizzly bear was coming at me, teeth bared and claws ready for an attack. Another time, I dreamed that a large aircraft was making a landing. Suddenly, the plane crashed and began rolling toward me.

The recurring dreams that stayed with me the most were definitely not something I would wish on anyone. They were more like nightmares and they always orbited my former house on Center Rd. As a result, I began to think of the place as center rd. house. I am no expert, but it does not take a big leap to understand why my malicious dreams involved the center rd. house. Obviously, my mind remained trapped in that place with a scattering of skeletons hidden within its walls. Mind you, I had long ago moved out of that house. There was nothing wrong with the house, but my dreams always took place in that house. Similar to some hauntings, the fiendish dreams of that house attached itself to me. My life improved, surroundings changed, and my spiritual life grew, but because I deliberately chose not to face the root of what truly troubled me, my dreams shadowed me across space and time.

Each dream started out the same. I would walk around the house and check each window and door to make sure we were safe and secure. However, with no apparent reason, the minute I locked the next window, the previous one turned up unlocked. When I went back to lock it again, it looked broken, and the wood frame appeared twisted as if someone had forced it open from the outside. Sometimes the dream shifted to primarily the doors and same thing happened with the front door twisting in along the top corner and the door lock broken. With another shift within the dream, I would discover that the back garage door was standing wide open. I would quickly shut it and begin to secure it with the bolt and find the locking mechanism lying on the floor. Sometimes the images shifted and the garage became a basement where the back door led outdoors. However, the theme was the same.

At some point, the dream progressed to shadowy figures attempting to get in. Other times, the shadowy figures appeared to be taunting me as they easily broke locks and twisted windows and doors. It was as if they were letting me know that I was not safe, nor secure. They wanted me to know that they could easily get in whenever they had a whim. In one such dream, the figures flung the garage door aside on their way out with me hiding behind the freezer. I could hear them laughing as they walked away. In another dream, the shadowy figure threw a rock through my daughter's upstairs bedroom window, indicating once again that I was not safe, nor would I ever be safe.

The intrusion of these unsettling dreams was taking a toll on me and I needed to make sense of it all. At some point, a thought came to me that it might be worth a try to find out why an unconscious problem was making an effort to reveal itself to my conscious self. With time, I began to see a pattern. Recognizable images in some of the dreams coincided with what was going on in my life. Stress seemed to trigger a dream when emotions were raw between my abuser and me. The library helped me with a search for answers. While there, I came across a book that had to do with dreams. While my children were deep into their book, I settled down to read a little bit before heading back to Center rd. house.

There was a valid reason I did not feel safe. If I understood correctly, my house symbolized my inner spirit. When someone dreams about a home, it usually denotes a place of refuge where basic needs like love thrive and where moral values reign. Since my dream continually put forth a house broken into, it suggested to me that I was feeling disrupted, possibly by a specific relationship or recent situation. Some facet of me that I have starved was trying to reveal itself. Perhaps that starved facet of me was the piece of evidence that my basic needs were not being met, I was not feeling loved, and my values were attacked by outside forces. As for continually checking security measures, I learned that the action of locking doors and windows suggest an inner fear and low self-worth. It also suggests that I am cautious about letting others in out of fear of exposing my true emotional state.

I certainly learned more about me in that short span of reading. It was like a light coming on and chasing away the creatures of the dark. To be aware of the truth can be quite empowering. Still, I certainly had a lot of work ahead of me if I wanted to gain a better understanding of my inner self. At least, I no longer dreaded going to sleep as much as before.

Nevertheless, the empowering feeling did not make the dreams go away. It took a while but I finally came to terms that my inner self was sick. I knew this because the symptoms showed themselves within each dream so the root of the problem could surface. It hit me that I was not at peace, my anxiety level was up, my emotional state was suffering, and I required relief. To guard my heart from breaking under the load of this inner sickness, I had to go to the only One who loves me more than I will ever comprehend, the Lord.

"Keep your heart with all diligence, for out of it is the wellspring of life." (Proverbs 4:23) World English Bible (WEB)

*****

The cosmic universe reveals that there is something much bigger than we are that something is God and He created us. He supplies His grace and power to forgive our sins once we acknowledge them; therefore, it is reasonable to believe that He can heal our spirit when it is ailing. To do this, He desires a personal relationship with us. All He asks is that He be the first we go see for advice, when sick, when in doubt, when feeling lost, and when we have erred. By doing so, the cleansing of our spirit can take place.

"You shall serve Yahweh your God, and he will bless your bread and your water, and I will take sickness away from among you." (Exodus 23:25)World English Bible (WEB)

*****

This next dream appeared long after my move from the center rd. house, but it was entirely different from the previous dreams. The dream came at the same time as I was grieving the death of my brother, so I suspected an important mystery for me to solve.

In the dream, I find myself confronting a stormy day with thunderous clouds darkening the sky. The path I am on is narrow, winding, and hindered by a roots and rugged terrain. I want to rest for a while, but a fierce wind cuts through me like a knife. The rain and fierce wind begin to push and assault my body. With each assault, a feeling of weariness, sorrow, and hopelessness rears its head. I am alone in my pain.

For a moment, a seething anger takes control, over the loss of what was. The next instant an icy chill takes hold in my bones for what I had to endure. Numbness seeps in for a visit only because winter is already making its home in this place. Looking around I see that the coming darkness is settling upon me like a blanket and I accept that I have a hole of emptiness growing deep inside, so it must mean that my heart is either broken or it is dying. *Would anyone notice if my heart were to wither away?*

How can I get past this pain? Struggling to my feet, I begin to fight my way through this desolate terrain and I fear that I might not be able to find my way. Reaching for something to hold onto, I notice that there is nothing to grab. I so want to find relief from this lonely despair! Pulling my wrap tight for protection, I recall the reason I am here and I cry out at the wind. *Does hope even exist? Is there anyone I can turn to?* In an instant, I awaken from the dream coated with a clammy sweat along with rapid breathing. In this defining moment, the questions and the answers begin to emerge. On bended knee beside my bed, I bow my head and begin to pray; *oh Lord God, I need you. Please, hear my prayer and help me!*

"Hear, Yahweh, my righteous plea; Give ear to my prayer, that doesn't go out of deceitful lips." (Psalm 17:1) World English Bible (WEB)

IMITATION OF LOVE

It was time to look back to those long forgotten places hidden in the corners of my mind. Through scripture, I read that God has a plan for me. Therefore, I began my search in the buried memories to help me learn and grow.

Long before meeting the people along life's crossroad, bringing dramatic change into my life, I recall a simpler time when all seemed joyful and safe. I knew that all was well and that my parents loved me, almost as much as God does. Our family laughed, cried, but always loved one another.

Thinking about my family brought up a pleasant memory about the time we had stopped on a trip and I took my eyes off Daddy for a moment. Suddenly, I saw him at a food counter and quickly ran up and grabbed his arm for assurance that everything was okay. You see, my father and my mother gave me a sense of a stability and well-being. My dad was my protector. Looking back with adult eyes, I can now see why I felt that way at the time, because our parents are an earthly reflection of the Heavenly Father. Parents are a special reminder about our Creator and His protecting love, healing love, and eternal love.

Despite our human frailties and trivial misunderstandings, our family accepted one another and quick to forgive. We occasionally engaged in modest disagreements, but never did we quarrel. As individuals, each of us reacted according to our own strengths and limitations to the tie that held us together as a family who loved God. Yet circumstances had a hand at laying out the groundwork about my own role in my future abuse. Since childhood, my character has been that of a sensitive and caring person who tends to consider the needs of others. As a result, I offered no serious threat to forceful individuals that might someday cross my path. As if in preparation for the eventual encounter with my abusers, I naively tempered my views so as not to hurt somebody's feelings. I reasoned that everyone's ideas and attitudes might differ, but we were all seeking friendship. Due to my lack of skill in the art of arguing, I avoided arguments by suggesting a compromise. If that did not go so good, then I removed myself, hoping the problem would sort itself. The hesitancy to engage in quarrels ultimately created a condition of feeling secondary among my peers. I sensed that my input was not appreciated, which affected my self-image.

As a young teenager, I was seeking independence. Like Pinocchio, I wandered and lost my way by way of someone whom I sought as a friend. With her faulty influence, we got into a little trouble. This was another step toward that fateful crossroad where abuse waited.

Meanwhile, I enjoyed attending worship services at an old steeple church in town. There were activities such as choir and youth groups where my friends and I could connect each Sunday. It was there that my parents had me baptized and later confirmed and it was there that I learned many memorable hymns such as the one about how *Jesus Loves Me and the one about climbing Jacob's ladder.* The old steeple church stands out in memory because it was there where I learned about Jesus and how He gave his life for me. Nevertheless, I was still unaware that I could have a personal relationship with this Triune God. I would find out so much more about Him later on.

Junior high school was upon me and I was shy around boys. However, by eighth grade I had developed a crush. The thing that did it for me was when I looked into a certain boy's eyes. They sparkled with humor, especially when he smiled. He was a year younger, but that did not matter. The extent of our relationship was holding hands, a smidgen of a peck on the cheek and passing notes to each other between classes. We occasionally talked by phone, but kept the calls short. He asked me to go steady and we became a twosome for several months. Then, one day he unexpectedly broke up with me by way of a note. I did not know the core reason at that time. The next fall, a friend of the boy delivered a note to me on behalf of him, asking if we could try again. The note spelled out that someone had spread an unkind rumor about me, causing him to ask for his friendship ring back. Somewhat hesitant, I finally agreed to try again and we went back to writing notes and calling each other until it was time for me to move on to High School. I soon came to realize that we were slowly drifting apart because we attended different schools and rarely found time to talk. After considering, I broke up with him by way of the most logical method, a note. Nevertheless, we stayed casual friends. I slowly came to understand that the main purpose of the relationships in my youth were to teach me about choices.

Life presents us with choices every day and with each choice comes a lesson to absorb or to ignore. The lesson learned here was that God desires us to follow His path, but He also gives us free will. When we choose to take our own path, we are at risk of losing our way and making mistakes thus ending up in a place with bittersweet or even disastrous consequences.

"Thus says Yahweh, Stand you in the ways and see, and ask for the old paths, where is the good way; and walk therein, and you shall find rest for your souls: but they said, we will not walk [therein]." (Jeremiah 6:16) World English Bible (WEB)

High school was fine. Not used to so many people and the frantic pace, I shied away from joining any select groups. At the most, I counted maybe a half a dozen friends. My junior year was a bit more interesting because I was familiar with the busy schedule. Dating did not seem overly important because I was focusing on my grades. However, I admit that I went on a couple of practice dates with a boy who was a casual friend. Something awakened in me when I entered my senior year. I became more interested in dating, especially since most of my friends had boyfriends.

My path was leading me ever closer to the crossroad where I would meet my future abuser. Would I have gone out with him if I could foresee the future? I will never know.

We met at a community dance and spent most of the evening dancing, talking, and exchanging phone numbers. I was surprised when he called me several weeks later, asking me to his school dance. He was nice, had a sense of humor, and was polite to me and to my parents. Our relationship grew and we went steady.

Unconscious attitudes follow all of us and mine was viewing the world through invisible colored glasses. I talked myself into believing that what we had was real. I trusted my own conception of reality and tuned out questioning thoughts. He seemed loyal to his family, but he also gave me a ring that had belonged to his old girlfriend. He borrowed my car, broke the transmission, and never offered to help fix it. I wanted to see what I desired instead of listening to my conscience, thereby tuning out God.

"Trust in Yahweh with all your heart, and don't lean on your own understanding." (Proverbs 3:5) World English Bible (WEB)

After high school graduation, I began attending a trade school full-time. Around the same time, the young man I had been dating suggested that we become more serious by proposing marriage. I accepted. Soon after, he began to pressure me to take our relationship to a new level. His thought was that he loved me and if I loved him, I should prove it by giving myself to him.

I was petrified. I knew nothing about bedroom stuff except for the basics taught in school and at home. I did not want to take this path, but naive as I was, I did not know how to handle the situation. If only I had asked someone's advice, but I was afraid to talk to anyone. I felt alone with nowhere to turn for guidance. Unfortunately, I neglected to talk to God. Anguish consumed me so I had forgotten to turn to Him. He would have been able to guide me back on the right path. Because I chose the wrong path, I ended up feeling forced to give in.

Being innocent, I was not ready for what happened. I was too young and the experience was not pleasant. For a month, I waited, fretting silently that I might have become pregnant, because lack of protection. I knew that since I gave in once, he would expect me to give in again. From then on, I found many excuses to put off having relations, which was a happy relief.

The decision to give in to my boyfriend led me onto a side path that I would regret traveling. In addition, it turned out to contain rough terrain with ominous warning signs, but I failed to see them.

Like a kitten into a lion's den, I wandered blindly ahead with no idea of what lay beyond.

I envisioned myself on a path to a good future with a man I cared for. He came home on leave from the Army for a week so we could be married. All went well and we both enjoyed our time together again. While at the reception, he was sociable, his charm drew people to him, and that pleased him and me. Subsequently, my rose-colored glasses got in the way again. I was unprepared for what happened next. For our hastily planned honeymoon, my folks drove their trailer to a county park. We drove there after the reception. The morning after our arrival, my husband became mad because I would not go find a store to buy him cigarettes. Then he complained about the lack of space in the trailer and wished that I had spent money on a hotel room. He made himself so agitated that he pushed me up against the screen door with enough force that I fell out on my backside. I was ready to end the honeymoon and we headed back to my folks house until his departure.

Never have I encountered such abnormal behavior. The man I married was nothing like the man I first met. It was as if he had gone through some kind of metamorphism and turned into an entirely different person eerily similar to Dr. Jekyll and Mr. Hyde. For those of you who do not know, Dr. Jekyll and Mr., Hyde, the term describes two distinct personalities. Never being acquainted with an abuser before now, I did not recognize the signs, but they were there. He was polite and amiable, quite smart, but he knew how to work people. He presented different persons' in the public eye versus the privacy of the home. Over time, I would begin to recognize the contrasts between the man I first met and this two-person man. I saw the power struggle, the jealousy, controlling behavior, his unrealistic expectations, and placing blame on others.

"There is one who speaks rashly like the piercing of a sword, But the tongue of the wise heals.." Proverbs 12:18 World English Bible (WEB)

By week's end, my new husband shipped out for overseas deployment in Vietnam for a year. While waiting for him to return, I landed a new job in my trade and saved much of my paycheck since I lived with my parents. I wrote to him often and he answered back but not as often. I reasoned that the mail delivery took longer due to his far away location. Occasionally, he would send a little money for me to save for him and even sent me a gift for Christmas. Meanwhile, my imaginings of an idealistic marriage continued.

Five months passed by with letters flowing back and forth. When I saw reports of fighting, I worried that he might be in the midst of danger. A couple of months into the New Year, I received news that he would go on rest and recuperation leave in Hawaii. We were to meet there and spend a week in paradise together. Most of what I had saved went for airfare and motel lodgings. I was looking forward to seeing him again. The beach and surroundings were beautiful and we enjoyed hours of exploring them together.

While there, my husband did not appear to be concerned about the cost of anything and advised me to rent a car, so there was an extra expense paid for with my savings. He reminded me that he would need his money when he returned to duty.

A fellow soldier and his girlfriend joined us on our drive around the island. As we spent more time together, I noticed odd behavior. He would occasionally be quiet and short tempered when the other two were elsewhere. When the others were around, he would be friendlier. I did not know what the problem was, but guessed it was war stress and decided to let it go. The Holy Spirit whispered, *wrong move Kathy.* Why was I hanging onto to denial? His behavior was clearly a sign of something amiss.

Two weeks later, I received a distressing letter. My husband had contracted a venereal disease from an encounter with a paid escort. The disease had gone undetected until after his return to duty. In the letter, he apologized and informed me that I should see a doctor. This news was shocking! Not only was I upset about almost catching a disease, but also the thing that hurt most was that he had been unfaithful to our oath by having relations with other women.

My dreams shattered right before my eyes and I had now felt the shabbier side of life! In the moment of this pain, the only thing that came to me was a phrase, although I did not know its origin, *if you lie down with dogs, you get up with fleas.*

At first, I screamed, and then I cried. I hated that his actions brought pain. Unsure about what to do next, I took a chance and turned to God. I was unsure on what to say so I tested God by demanding Him to put some sense into my husband's head or else punish him. I know God sees me and hears me, but He does not wish for us to make demands of Him. He must have a lot of patience especially with me.

I needed to talk to someone discreetly, though I dreaded talking about the despicable situation I was in with just anyone. After a pause, I chose to share what happened with my parents. Dad was livid. Mom was furious and both shared their opinions. Dad included info that involved treatment for such diseases in his time. They said I had grounds for a divorce, but left it up to me. All I knew was that I wanted to sort it all out before making a decision. With no sign of disease, as a precaution the doctor prescribed medication.

The more I thought about the situation the angrier I became. This anger led me down one more side road. I decided to attend a drinking party near the overhead power lines. I wanted to forget my pain with beer. While my friend was talking to someone else, a young man came over. I greeted him and we talked under the stars for a while. We both shared about ourselves. In the midst, he asked what was bothering me. I mumbled the minimum about was bothering me.
At no time did anything happen.

A week later, my husband's brother-n-law came over and accused me of committing adultery. I sure did not see that coming! I was deeply offended that he would accuse me unjustly with a false accusation. The accusation hurt me to the core and I let him know it heatedly.

The brother-in-law said he learned about our encounter because he worked with the young man. The best I can figure is that the young man told him a made-up story. This brother-n-law went on to say that he had written my husband about my adultery. I told him that was fine, because I knew and God knew my honesty when I said nothing happened. My brother-n-law did not accept my truth. In the midst of our argument, I did not reveal my husband's infidelity and contraction of a disease. I still had not decided about our marital state, so the less other people knew the better.

At no time during the rest of his tour did my husband confront me in any of his letters, so I presumed my brother-n-law's threat was a bluff. However, whenever I visited my husband's folks, my brother-n-law and sister-n-law looked at me it was with aloofness.

Looking back at the encounter, I asked myself how I ended up here with a family member not trusting me. Why did the young man lie about our encounter? Could I have given the wrong signal? I was not in the habit of going to beer gatherings, but I began to regret going at all. It was an awakening of how my actions produced consequences beyond my imagination. I knew I did not want to go down this road, all because of my anger and pain. I needed to let go of this anger and talk to my husband. Due to the war, a letter was the only form of communication. It took time to compose what I wanted to say, but in due course, I finished it and mailed it off. At the conclusion of the heart-wrenching letter, I agreed to give him another chance due to God's infinite capacity to forgive me.

"Let all bitterness, wrath, anger, outcry, and slander, be put away from you, with all malice. And be kind to one another, tenderhearted, forgiving each other, just as God also in Christ forgave you." Ephesians 4:31-32 World English Bible (WEB)

From this point, I sincerely desired to follow God's path. Aiming for the right path led me on a personal journey of faith. For a person who was an irregular worshiper, I applied my faith irregularly in a meaningful way. It was time for change. Thus began a new ritual of learning how to pray every night and morning. It was difficult at first. Sometimes I would forget, other times I would make excuses but then I was still a rather new at this.

To understand the scriptures better, I took on a project of reading the entire bible. I found my bible, began with the book of Genesis, and continued all the way through Revelation. It took a long time to complete and some of the reading was a bit dry with the word 'begot' used so often. However, I felt that what I was learning was well worth the effort and quite an adventure.

SEEING THE TRUTH

Dedication is one of my traits, because I diligently maintained an effort to save our marriage. His duty in Vietnam ended, but there were no welcome-home parades. Instead, he returned with the knowledge that a number of people did not care about the returning vets. They did not want the soldiers involved in the Vietnam conflict. He returned feeling frustrated. He also had the mistaken idea that he was still single. I could see something dark shadowing him. I did not know enough about post war stress but still guessed that it might be the problem. As a result, I gave him time to readjust. We settled in a small apartment near my job and he found work with the state highway roadworks.

We started by becoming reacquainted. At first, we got along fine. After a while, I noticed stress flowing from him. It led him to spew hateful words my way. After he calmed down, he returned to being nice again. Then he would revert to being spiteful. It was maddening being around him during his episodes. Even worse was how to predict when he might change. It was as if he was stuck on an endless roller coaster ride. He refused to seek counseling, so I changed my routine so I could steer clear if he was having an episode, so as not to irate him. Sadly, my timing was off one night. I wanted to treat him to a new recipe that he might like. Instead, he took one taste and yelled, **not even pigs would eat this slop.** He slammed the plate on the counter and walked out.

Little by little, I began to doubt myself. That was when my internal voice began having an internal conversation. *What happened? Did I do something wrong? No, you did not. He said I was worthless. No, he has the problem. This does not make any sense. Married couples do not behave this way.*

I wanted to believe that our romance life was okay, although he ignored me sometimes. I suspected that he was not content. I too felt it was not what I had envisioned. One sizable obstacle was his desire for unusual bedroom activity, which did not fit my moral compass. Some of his whims were too extreme. Sometimes, immediately after a verbal or mental tirade, he would force me to have relations with him. It felt like one more form of assault right after the earlier one. He kept up pressuring me to engage in his unusual activity, until he realized that I would never give in.

Unexpectedly, I discovered I was pregnant. I was happy. I had longed for a baby to nurture and love. I could now begin preparing for this new life. Many times, I thought about names and what gender the baby might be. Before my shape changed, I suffered through the morning sickness. Several times, it came on while driving to work and I would have to pull over until the nausea settled. Then the morning sickness stopped and kept working throughout my pregnancy. Baby and I waited joyfully for his or her entrance to this world.

I was not entirely sure that my husband was as excited as I was about this new life. He seemed unsettled that it would change everything, and he was certainly right.

As the months flew by, my belly grew and my husband said he could not stand looking at me in any more. I replied *excuse me! You are the one who caused me to look this way*. This made him mad and he stormed out. The endless roller coaster ride continued and his disparaging words gradually wore me down and ate away my self-value. I turned to God for answers and knew that he was there, but I still felt sad and alone. I believe that in my sorrow, he was carrying me through the muck.

"Why are you in despair, my soul? Why are you disturbed within me? Hope in God! For I shall still praise him for the saving help of his presence." (Psalm 42:5) World English Bible (WEB)

Two months before the birth, we bought a small house and I prepared for this new baby. I was in my ninth month and the area was in the midst of an icy winter storm. One morning, I asked my husband to take out the garbage before waste management came.

Notorious for forgetting, he left for work in hurry. The large bag was still sitting by the door. I shook my head, and began attempting to maneuver not only the heavy bag but my misshapen body as well. If anything could go wrong, it would on my watch. Down I went with a splat on the ice. The pain in my ankle was unbearable. Not able to get up, I began to crawl. Slowly and painfully, I crawled back inside. The sight of a pregnant woman crawling on the ice packed snow must have looked laughable. However, I was in no laughing mood. I was furious with my husband, so I called my folks for help. After saying that the baby was okay and describing my ankle injury, my mother concluded that it was not broken. My husband was not helpful, so my father took me to the doctor. Two weeks later, I gave birth to a healthy daughter with my foot wrapped in a bandage.

Time passed and our baby became a toddler. For a time, this little girl improved her daddy's disposition. Yet, he was of the mindset that his money was for him first, then his daughter, and me last. Then another dark change appeared. Not interested in listening to reason, his abusive behavior increased to a new level. When our toddler was at the babysitter, He threw the kitchen drawers on the floor and demanded that I clean it up. Then he got his unloaded musket loader out and threatened to shoot me. After watching him pack the gun previously, I knew I would have time to get away. I was upset and yet the scenario appeared comical. Suddenly, I burst out with laughter. This made him even more furious and he went to the kitchen, picked up a knife, and came after me. I ran and hid until I saw him leave. He returned the next day teeming with apologies.

The next time his violence blew was when he threw my keys on top of the roof so I could not leave. Later, when he had calmed down, he once again apologized. This time he promised that he would never behave like that again. Then he pressured me to forgive him and so I appeased him.

God only knows why I forgave him. I hoped he was sincere, but I also asked God to hear my silent prayer. Life went on with its difficulties as I persevered to keep some form of normalcy. Then I learned that I was pregnant with our second child. As my belly grew, so did my husband's rude comments about my shape.

Around the same time, I heard about a small church nearby. I wanted to check it out, but my husband refused to go with me, so my daughter, along with some of the family, began worshiping there. I fell in love with the friendly people and the new pastor. One Sunday, while in prayer, an image appeared behind my closed eyelids. Jesus was watching me with outstretched arms and a smile. It became clear to me that this place was where I belonged.

Halfway through my pregnancy, something occurred that changed things again. For years, I suspected that my husband had been seeing women in secret. I never had proof and when questioned he always denied it. This time I had proof. When confronted, he at first denied it. When he could not deny any longer, he explained that he needed more than one woman. He argued that I drove him to do it and that I should be more understanding. My answer to him was, *do right by your children and me. Straighten up or move out.*

It did not take him long to make his decision. He confronted me with a false accusation that I had been unfaithful. He argued that the child was not his and he packed his things and walked out. His action was a betrayal of our marriage vow and an act of abandonment.

Five months later, he came back on bended knee, displaying tears. He begged me to take him back with a promise to be a better father and husband. I gave in for the children's sake, but when trust is broken, any amount of repair may not be enough.

A bit wary, I suspected that his evenings out were a bit too cagey. Then the bottom fell out when my husbands' hidden stash of money turned up missing. He planned to use it during reserve training. He accused me of being a thief, screaming with rage. Glaring at him, I denied his false charge. As I walked away in disgust, he came up from behind and gave me a kidney punch that sent me sprawling to the floor in pain. Without making sure I was all right, he left to join his reserve group. I did not hear from him for two weeks. My body hurt so bad it took all my strength to get in bed. My daughter took over, looking after her younger brother while I rested. He had me so brainwashed into believing that no one would believe me if I reported him. When he assaulted me, I did not call the police.

I never shared any of this with anyone, but somehow my grandmother seemed to know something was amiss. I went to visit her while she was recuperating in the hospital. She opened up to me about her own abuse. She shared that as a young wife and mother, she too had dealt with an abusive husband. She found her own answer through the words of her Savior, Jesus Christ. She quoted to me from memory, the following scripture.

"Jesus replied, "love the Lord your God with all your heart and with all your soul and with all your mind. This is the first and greatest commandment, and a second is like it: Love your neighbor as yourself" Matthew 22:37-39 World English Bible (WEB)

Grandma explained that God wants us to love him with all our heart and all our soul along with loving our neighbor. Yet, if we do not love ourselves as well, we are not fulfilling Jesus' commandment. It was her words along with comprehending what the scripture meant when it all became clear. If I continued to live with someone who continually mistreated me along with his unfaithfulness, I did not love myself. This was a hard lesson to digest. Eventually, I came to realize that it was time walk away, so I filed for divorce. I knew this was the right decision, although I still felt lost. What I found though was a loving God who was present in my darkness, revealing a new path.

"When you pass through the waters, I will be with you; and through the rivers, they shall not overflow you: when you walk through the fire, you shall not be burned, neither shall the flame kindle on you." (Isaiah 43:2) World English Bible (WEB)

*****

Looking back to that time in my life, I now see that I was more in love with the idea of being in love. In actuality, I had no idea about the meaning of true mutual love; a covenant based on trust and a bond as God intended.

"Beloved, let us love one another, for love is of God; and everyone who loves is born of God, and knows God" 1 John 4:7 World English Bible (WEB)

A NEW STORM DESCENDS

Abilities as a single parent were sometimes in doubt. Was I too easy or was I too strict? As the sole wage earner now, I was a touch tense. Were the children's needs being met? Did I instill plenty of good values? Did I effectively teach them about how precious they are to God? Did I teach them to seek the essential things in life while they reach for the stars? I hope so. Just as a lighthouse carefully guides ships through unsafe waters so does a parent for their children. God knows my heart. He knows where I can improve and if I am willing to listen and obey.

Being a single parent meant no adult to talk with as the children slept. Many nights I laid on the bed with exhaustion; emotional and physical. I questioned how long I could keep up with the loneliness and uncertainty. I worried about taking care of the children's needs, cleaning the house, cooking, chopping wood for the freestanding stove, and the other daily chores. It was during those times, I leaned a bit more on my Heavenly Father to lighten my burdens. Maybe the house was not spotless, but I was doing okay.

Considering that I was no longer in a dysfunctional relationship, I had the mistaken idea that my mental state was better. I discounted a recommendation from a well-meaning associate. She told me that many times after a woman leaves an abuser, she steps into a new relationship without addressing her own weaknesses. Unless she faces her liabilities so she can make changes, she will end up in a similar or worse relationship. I declined her advice because I thought I was ready to socialize again.

A storm was descending and I was unprepared. Blindness clouded my vision, so I did not grasp what the Lord was revealing. As a result, I was heading toward another crossroad where a new abuse waited.

Once again, someone with unrestrained mental issues would target me. He engineered himself into my life and his chronic mental issues would profoundly affect my family.

While working at a manufacturing company, a co-worker and I decided to carpool to and from work to cut down on fuel expenses. A month went by when he introduced me to a friend of his. The man appeared to be kind, cordial, and showed an affectionate sort of charm. I believed that my co-worker to be reliable when he said this man was a good person. The man showed consideration for my point of view and feelings, which triggered something in me, and my distrust began to lessen.

We shared our history stories and that is when I learned he had been in jail, for being involved in a fight. It would be much later before the truth came out, but it would happen after I began genuinely caring for him and dedicated to our relationship.

Given time, our relationship grew closer. Yet, I saw a small glimpse of odd behavior on his part that he had hoped I would not notice. From normal observation, I could see that he was extremely fastidious about his grooming habits, but threw cigarette butts all over the yard and then expected the children to pick the butts up as a chore. He was a perfectionist when it came to neatness among his own personal items. He even attempted to pressure me to accept his management style over my homes' neatness. I declined to give in, because his method of cleanliness was overly institutional. After living with abuse and how it disparages a person, the thought of submission meant something bad. I noticed a few times when I felt a bit uncomfortable with some romantic suggestions, but what did I know, I only had an ex-husband as a comparison. I did know that this man never yelled or beat me, so I let go of any wariness. Maybe it was because I still had trust issues.

Time passed, then one day while at work I received a call with shocking news that the police had arrested him for exposing himself at a middle school. I was stunned and the news was hard to bear alone, so I quickly turned to my family and pastor for counseling. We struggled to try to understand who this man was and why he felt compelled to expose him to adolescents. With disbelief, I hoped counseling might lead to eventual recovery.

After serving his time, he claimed that he regretted his crime and had sought God's word through scripture. He was repentant and wanted to be a better man. Therefore, he began attending weekly group counseling, private counseling, became involved in church, and individual bible study. Gradually, he confided that his parents were alcoholics and that as a child, he had submitted to someone's will. The person was an adult male seeking sensual gratification. Not understanding this mental disorder, I sought out his counselor. The limited amount I learned was that he started out using voyeurism to satisfy an urge. Then he graduated to exhibitionism. I wanted to believe that he could beat this compulsion, so I boosted him with God's word.

Even though he professed his faith and received baptism, he fell back into old habits of isolating himself, allowing his inner demons to gain control. When he was this way, a visible change came over him. His eyes seemed to turn into shark's eyes, glassy and emotionless. He then concealed his behavior and gave into temptation. Sadly, an offence took place against another adolescent. I was surprised to learn that the authorities only kept him in jail for two weeks. The courts reduced his offence from a felony to a misdemeanor and the court ordered him to continue with probation along with proposed counseling. It seemed to me that the justice system had failed by just slapping him on the hand and not addressing his deep-rooted mental disorder.

1. Voyeurism is a term that describes watching an unsuspecting or unwilling person who might be in various stages of disrobing.
2. Exhibitionism types II and I is a term that describes exposing one's own genitalia to a person that is not expecting a show. Type I is a typical flaccid exposer; type II is a sociopath exposer who may have a history of other abnormal behavior.

Because of his bizarre obsession, he victimized many innocent children and destroyed the trust of many. Attempting to make sense of this sort of sin, I researched and found an article about Pedophilia. Something about the description deeply disturbed me. It described someone with a deviant desire of sensual activity with a preteenager.

Reading those words triggered a flash inside my mind. I thought back and questioned every moment when he was around my children. Why did he roam the house that time in the night, in the nude? Why was he determined to befriend via tickling or wrestling one child? I began to see him in a new light. Had he been attempting to groom my children to be a victim? I knew that I needed to arm myself with knowledge about predators.

Extremely troubled, I encouraged each child to speak freely. I assured them that they were not in trouble. Then I gently asked if he had ever touched them inappropriately or spied on them when they were undressing. Both questions brought a no. You need to know that my children held different temperaments. One child was forceful and pushed back often. The other was a bit more reserved. Because of this, I had some unease. Later on, they both told me that they felt uncomfortable whenever he was near them.

I heard somewhere that when helping a child open up it is best if one does not looking directly at the child and vice versa. Years later, one child, now an adult, opened up after I approached the subject again by talking about the original edition of this book. I wondered aloud if this child wanted to share some thoughts about the past. I drove while my adult child began to open up. There was an admission that the man did do something, but my child did want to speak further about it. I was not about to force this child to relive what happened, but I apologized for allowing the man into our lives.

I deeply regret that I had not been more cautious stepping into the relationship. If only I had detected the hidden signs. He used exploitation, manipulation, and submission in an attempt to attain a sensual fantasy. Later, I came to realize that he was destined struggle in the wilderness of sin until he fully surrendered himself to God.

What happened next was disturbing, though unverifiable. I insisted that he not call, yet the phone would ring regularly, with no one on the other end except the sound of breathing. Seconds later, the person hung up. In the night, someone punctured two tires on my car. Next, someone threw a rock through the upstairs bedroom window. Lastly, some yard tools disappeared from the backyard.

The effect on my nerves triggered a series of nightmares nearly every night. I kept seeing him befriending two children and me picking up a shard of broken glass intending to cause him harm as a way to stop him from preying on the children. For my sanity, these dreams had to stop, so I reached out to God for comfort.

Lying under the bed covers in the darkness of night, I silently hoped that answers might come. The hope I sought came through a simple prayer where I laid all of my sin at the cross of my Savior, Jesus Christ. In return, the unseen Companion covered me with His grace. I felt His love encircle me and felt at peace.

The harassment finally stopped along with the weird dreams. I began to grasp that through all of my worst moments, my Lord and Savior never left my side. I knew He loved and forgave me. He is a God of glory, reassurance, and strength.

After reading more scriptures, a new understanding emerged. God was making a promise to me every day. When I was scared, he was protecting me. When I was weary, he was comforting me. When I fell, he picked me up. Jesus Christ's words are true, eternal, and waiting for me, waiting for all, with a desire for a relationship. Because of this, I no longer want to lean on my own understanding. Instead, I lean on His promises, because His words are speaking to me. I know that He will never let me down, nor leave me. This Bible verse has helped encourage and comfort me many times. I hope it may help you too.

"But we have this treasure in clay vessels that the exceeding greatness of the power may be of God, and not from ourselves. We are pressed on every side, yet not crushed; perplexed, yet not to despair; pursued, yet not forsaken; struck down, yet not destroyed; always carrying in the body the putting to death of the Lord Jesus, that the life of Jesus may also be revealed in our body." 2 Corinthians 4:7-10 World English Bible (WEB)

※※※※

When the term 'submission,' comes up, many faith led people rely on the Bible. Submission means respectful compliance to another. For a victim of abuse, the word 'submission' means something different. Most victims have a tainted perception along with dark visualizations due to their abuser using power and control to force their will on the other. The result is a crushed spirit. If one looks at the Greek word for submission, one will find that it means an attitude of loyalty, support, and cooperation. This description is similar to our relationship with God. God does not mistreat, belittle, exploit, or manipulate for God is love in its purest state. Submission to a spouse, as God intended, must be a voluntary action between equals by complying with the other and vice versa. Since abuse is destructive, submitting to an abusive spouse would be identical to allowing the destructiveness to continue instead of taking action to break the cycle.

****

I wrote this letter to God after the devastating events leading up to the casualty of a relationship due to sin. The letter is about forgiveness.

Dear Heavenly Father, I feel empty inside and yet I ache deeply. Someone I loved and trusted has betrayed me and my heart is broken. The pain comes in waves, washing over me and leaving behind a shattered woman. He destroyed what we had by a senseless act. Because of that act, loved ones and I are in pain.

I have so many bewildering feelings. One moment I am seething with rage, other times I am sad for the loss of what was. I am exhausted. Help me Lord. How do I pick up the shattered pieces of so I can go on? Does he feel remorse? He apologized, but could not promise that nothing would happen again. He sees himself in a deep well. A rope is within reach but he does not grab for it.

The Bible reveals that your grace is love in action towards those who deserve the reverse of love. Because your grace is abundant, and we are weak, your power is made perfect. Father, please show me how to forgive just as you have forgiven me. If I can pardon his transgressions, I can then let go of my casting of blame. In so doing, I am releasing him to you.

Jesus Christ said that all things are possible through faith. I want to live by this faith and learn to trust again. With your abiding love and guidance, I pray for a better awareness of you. In Jesus name, Amen.

THIS IS MY SEASON

In retrospect, my past struggle in the wilderness was God's way of revealing Himself thru the poignant treasures within scripture. These lyrical words were composed long ago by someone of faith.

"For everything there is a season, and a time for every purpose under heaven: A time to be born, And a time to die; A time to plant, And a time to pluck up that which is planted; A time to kill, And a time to heal; A time to break down, And a time to build up; A time to weep, And a time to laugh; A time to mourn, And a time to dance; A time to cast away stones, And a time to gather stones together; A time to embrace, And a time to refrain from embracing; A time to seek, And a time to lose; A time to keep, And a time to cast away; A time to tear, And a time to sew; A time to keep silence, And a time to speak; A time to love, And a time to hate; A time for war, And a time for peace." Ecclesiastes 3:1-8 World English Bible (WEB)

As in the scripture, this is my season. It is a time to experience peace, joy and love in a new way as I continue on the path with my Savior. My conclusion is that every trial faced was for a purpose. I found that in my darkest moments, God is present. He will never relent until He holds my heart fully. He desires me to turn to Him with all of my problems. Trusting Jesus Christ, is a joy because He is the bringer of the water of life.

Facing my past abusive relationships may have been a difficult path, but not as difficult as spending years of my life in denial and refusing to consider how and why it happened. Confronting ones flaws brings vulnerability so it takes courage to explore the darkness of a broken past, but the embrace of the power of God's love is infinite.

Like the kneading of clay, I have been shaped, molded, and finally placed into the fire, all for what God intended. I feel as though I am reborn through my King, Jesus Christ. He is the cornerstone and as I stand upon his firm foundation, I am able to reach for the stars and explore the endless possibilities as I give myself to him for his glory!

Long ago, I did not know who I was. Now I am learning who I am. For someone who does not know Jesus, I am His reflection when I stand up for the weak, the abused, or the persecuted. I am His reflection when I cloth the poor and provide food for the hungry. I am His reflection when I share His living water with the thirsty.

"For I was hungry, and you gave me food to eat; I was thirsty, and you gave me drink; I was a stranger, and you took me in; naked, and you clothed me; I was sick, and you visited me; I was in prison, and you came to me." Matthew 25:35-36

*****

Grasping that I was depressed after my brother died was the start of another lasting promise of Gods' healing power. When I read my brother's obituary a spark ignited inside of me. I kept thinking about all of his accomplishments during his lifetime and then remembered what he said before he died; Kathleen, *do not sell yourself short, you need to believe in yourself.* I can still hear his voice in my mind. The sound of his voice was enough to lift my spirit. Holding onto memories and talking about him has kept him living in my heart. I know that the Triune God embraces him. Therefore, I chose to write about him, but God had another plan for me. God turned me around, put me on a path with a purpose. He was leading me on this exploration of my past abuse.

Life has mountaintops and valleys. It would be exhilarating if one could always be on the mountaintop close to heaven and our Creator. I am sure view is awe-inspiring, the fragrant breeze, cleansing. However, no one should stay on the summit indefinitely. Even Moses, after his encounter with God, came down from the mountain. He came down to be with his people so he might lead them as a group through the desert wilderness for forty years.

We must all face a wilderness on occasion. There will be marshes, dark valleys, desert, muck, and thirst. No one can go around any of it, because the path meanders through it all. Each of us must find our own way to reach God's firm ground.

I have been on that path and have experienced times that were unbearable. I know the feeling of failure, pain, and despair, but with God's embrace, I was able to get up and try again. Believing in the hope of something better, kept me going. Hope in a forgiving God who loves, unconditionally. That is why I identify with Moses and the Israelites' wilderness. God desired a relationship of trust with the Israelites, but they repeatedly tested Him, attempting to control Him, rather than rely on Him. I saw myself doing the same thing when I demanded that He fix my mistakes.

*****

Rest assured that whatever it is you might be facing, you are not alone. Jesus Christ loves you eternally. Whenever you are in unknown waters, He will be with you. He will never abandon you. He promises to be present all the days of your life if you let Him. He will carry you if you cannot stand. Give Him your trust and He will support you until you can reach firm ground and regain your strength

The Resurrected King took on our sins upon himself. He did this not to condemn us, but to save us. There is no greater love than this! My Lord came looking for me and knocked on my door because he has always loved me even before I took my first breath. He loves you too and desires to celebrate with you. He wants to bless your life and make it complete. He has extended an invitation to everyone for a relationship with Him.

"Behold, I stand at the door and knock. If anyone hears my voice and opens the door, then I will come in to him, and will dine with him, and he with me." (Revelation 3:20) World English Bible (WEB)

Jesus Christ shines down His pure grace and love when He embraces us. He may be a man, a son, a friend, a brother, a rabbi, a carpenter, a teacher, a prophet, but He is the Son of God. He paid the price for our sins by suffering greatly and then dying on the cross. In His suffering and death, He rose from the tomb and found peace and life again.

God released His Son to the cross, but also to the glory of resurrection. Like all fathers, His heart must have ached almost more than he could bear. Therefore, I believe He knows our pain. If we hope in the Resurrected Jesus, His living water will quench our thirst. We can then walk through any fire.

Looking at the cross reminds me of my own sin, and my own brokenness. Without Jesus to show the way, I would be stumbling in the dark with no hope of redemption. The empty cross and tomb is a reminder of My savior being raised up and defying death. He chose to be the sacrificial lamb for you and me because He has shown that in the end, He is the victor. The battle will continue until He returns, so until then, I will continue to trust that we can learn from the day of crucifixion and aspire to be better towards one another. God gives us that opportunity every day when He invites us to reach out to Him and receive His gift of eternal grace and love.

*****

I wrote this next piece long after my story came out. This is a letter for all abuse survivors.

Dear Survivor,

Today can be a new beginning if you so choose. You have the power to choose to stay paralyzed in the past or choose to move forward. Moving forward means discovering that what you went through is now over and that you are alive.

You have taken the first step to a wonderful new beginning. Maybe you are struggling to make sense of what happened or whether you could have prevented it. Please let that go and know that what happened to you was never your fault. If you are having trouble coping with jumbled feelings, please allow God to guide you as He can heal your mind and your inner spirit. I hope you know how much God loves you. If you turn to Him, He will reveal to you an inner strength, which is waiting to emerge.

You have already been brave, because you survived the nightmare.

Your inner spirit holds the same kind of courage as a mighty lion and that courage will now see you through the healing process.

In the meantime, you have probably built a cocoon around yourself as a way of coping with outside forces. If so, I am relieved because it means that you are giving time for a change to take place within you. When you are ready to emerge from your cocoon, you can cast off the old skin of fear, doubt, shame, and anger and become brand new, much like a beautiful butterfly.

No, you are not alone, because God is with you, I am with you and so is every other survivor. We all stand with you. From a survivor

'WOUNDED' POETRY COLLECTION
(And Bible Help)

I consider the arts to be a method of individual form of communication that is often times inspired by culture of our time. By itself, the arts are a natural display of the inner imaginative drive. The arts also help to bring change. The following poems are an expression of my view of the destructiveness and long-term effects of abuse and the wonder of God's grace giving hope for all.

Tragedy of Innocence

Playing joyfully on the hillside
While danger lurks so near,
They do not realize the anger,
Nor do they know of fear.

Hide and seek is their game
On this morn of new fallen rain.
Oh how young they are, these two.
Ignorant are they of the coming pain.

Gunshots are heard and all is still,
The hunters investigate their kill.
Two young fawns lying on the hill.

After the breakdown and ultimate end of our marriage, this poem was born. I was thinking about my children when I wrote it as I grasped the tragedy for them. Divorce leaves a lasting effect on children because they are the innocent ones.

A Cry in the Night

The cold, black of night
Touched my trembling fingertips.
How did I get here?
What did I do to deserve this?

I remember escaping
From a frightening blow.
The last words I heard was,
You reap what you sow.

With tear-filled eyes I ran,
But how far I could not say.
Then I fell upon the sand
And soon lost my way.

Fear filled my being
And I felt all alone.
I knew my heart was broken
and grew hard like a stone.

Looking to the sky,
I saw the brightening light.
It was my lighthouse
For my lack of sight.

A gentle voice beckoned
From the blue tinged sky,
Fear not dear child of mine,
You are loved, so no need to cry.

While recovering from the assault injury by my spouse, I wrote this poem, because it helped me make sense of the chaotic feelings crashing about inside of me, much like waves hitting against the rocks.

Sojourners' Tale

I am a traveler on this sphere called earth.
This is not my home so I continue my search.

The road I walk is the path of life,
Lured by illusions, yet pulled to the light.

Thunderous clouds darken the sky above.
Fear seeps in while stranded on this bluff.

The way is narrow and the rocks abound.
I sense many hazards all around.

The dangers that lurk, threatening my way,
are mostly obstacles that I have made.

I fight to break the bonds that hold me tight,
but the cause is lost, unless I give up the fight.

The source of hope is my persistent vision,
And to stay the course, my desired mission.

When I focus my eyes, the answer is clear,
My source of hope is Jesus my Savior.

He holds me close to ease my load,
offering living water to cleanse my soul.

He has loosened the bonds and set me free.
I wish to thank him for the gift He gave me.

Today I sing praises to God the most high.
He will never leave me all the days of my life.

So, when clouds are above, do not give into fear.
The sun's rays will shine through, because Jesus is near.

New Perspective

For every down, there is an up,
So when I stumble and I know I shall,
I will get back up.

For every cannot there is a can,
so when I fail as I surely will,
I shall try again.

For every tear shed, there is bravery too,
so when I've been hurt; it's a given fact,
I will smile through.

For every silence, there is sound,
so when the time is right to speak up,
I will abound.

For all the hate in the world, there is love,
so when hate arrives and it shall,
My heart will reach out with love from above.

Bible Help

God, the great Physician, makes us a promise every day. His promises come as a daily prescription filled with hope and healing. They are waiting for you in the Holy Bible.

When you worry;

Matthew 11: 28　　Psalm 55:22　　John 14:27

When you doubt;

Romans 8:28　　Psalm 31:24　　Mark 9:23

When you fear;

Isaiah 41:10　　Psalm 27:1　　Joshua 1:9

When you fail;

Psalm 145:14　　Proverbs 29:25　　2 Corinthians 4:8-9

When you are lonely;

John 14:18　　1 Peter 5:7　　Matthew 28:20

AFTERWORD

Considering what to do with my journal about enduring spousal abuse, the pastor at church presented a sermon that left a lasting impression with me. He included with the day's message, a question, and a challenge. He said, *'Jesus what are you doing here and how I can be a part of it?'*

For the next several weeks, I kept thinking about the significance of the challenge. Like a teasing itch that keeps coming back, an idea kept popping into my head. At first, I attempted to ignore it, but it would not leave. Consequently, I submitted my story to a publisher. The result was that the book became a reality, in its original state.

Since my brother was the bridge that led me to face the subject of abuse, I dedicated the original book (and this version too) to him, but God the Father, merits highest acknowledgment.

Towards the end of the publishing process, it dawned on me that the nightmares had ceased. I was so busy that I had not noticed. I believe the Holy Spirit had something to do with that. Finally, one more thing happened; an amazing dream came by for a visit.

*****

The light outdoors was extraordinarily vivid as my awareness intensified. What was most surprising was that I was sitting astride an enormous golden eagle and we were flying. The gentle breeze blew refreshingly through my hair, tossing my locks about. I was seeing everything with a new perspective as my gaze took in the fabulous view above, around, and below me. The meandering river resembled a snake winding along and the clouds almost near enough to touch. There was no fear in this place, only a feeling of being awestruck with exhilaration. Suddenly, I felt a pressure around my lower limb causing me to look down. Wrapped around my ankle was a heavy chain. As I was figuring out how to remove the chain, it slipped off, falling to the ground. In that instant, I realized that any burden I may have been carrying was gone and I was free. The next instant, I woke up with all of the vivid colors and visual imagery of the dream forever imprinted in my mind.

*****

My nightmares have never returned and I continue to reflect about the positive significance of the 'eagle dream' that materialized when it did. The dream was a defining moment and a lovely gift from God.

Does this sound impossible to you? It does not have to be—

"But he said, "the things which are impossible with men are possible with God.' Luke 18:27 World English Bible (WEB)

     God fulfills his promises every day as he provides his constant faithfulness. He knows me better than I know myself and he invites me to open my eyes and discover his plans for good relentlessly. He provides hope and a future with purpose. Every day God's word reveals new insight. His amazing grace inspires me to share my faith-inspired stories. In this way, I am honoring Him, as I continue to walk by faith with the Him.

    I have said enough about me. I am certain that everyone has a story of some kind of emotional pain, so I pray that my story may affirm that you are not alone. I hope that by sharing my testimony you might find help from the One who loves you most, the Lord.

"For God so loved the world, that he gave his one and only Son, that whoever believes in him should not perish, but have eternal life." JOHN 3:16 WORLD ENGLISH BIBLE (WEB)

    Jesus Christ bestowed His grace upon me by being present in my darkness and helping me close the door on the shadows. I was spiritually blind, but by believing in the Resurrected King, I can really see. From the cinders of failure, He is resurrecting me. Therefore, this is my testimony and my song of praise. Here I am Lord, at the foot of the cross, bowing in adoration and thankfulness for all that you have done for me and all humankind. On bended knee, I sing praise to your glory and power. Heaven is my true home and if God calls me home today; I shall dance before you Jesus, for you are my music, my song, and my vision. Amen

ABOUT THE AUTHOR

Hi, my name is Kathy Goodhew and I am a poet, illustrator, and writer of true and creative stories inspired by my faith. I am a published author of nonfiction and fiction books. They include a bird story about bullying for older children, a low-fantasy/science-fiction trilogy for young adults, and two printings about spousal abuse. Like so many of you, I wear many hats: I am a daughter, a sister, an aunt, a wife, a mother, and a grandmother. All of my hats have given me adventures, wild rides, and wonderful blessings.

My husband and I reside in a not-so-small town in the Pacific Northwest. In my neighborhood, those of us who live here can easily consider dodging rain a sport. Still, it is in this place that my heart truly thrives. I love the breathtaking mountain peaks, the grand forests, the pristine water, the abundant wildlife, and even the refreshing rain. My delight is our camping adventures in our motor home. I love to stroll along the beach in search of sea lions and eagles, and the sound of birds singing bring joy to my ears. Some of my pastimes include Poetry and sketching along with trying my hand at amateur photography. Reading fiction gives me great pleasure, which explains my interest in creative writing.

Lastly and most importantly, I am a follower of Jesus Christ and my desire is finding God's caress in His natural world and entwining them into my stories. Thank you for taking a walk with my thoughts.

Books:
1. A Vision Beyond Abuse 1st. and 2nd Edition
2. The Hidden Ones, Awakened (book 1)
3. The Hidden Ones, Confluence (book 2)
4. The Hidden Ones, Source (book 3)
5. Crow and Jay

For more information, please visit my website.
www.kathygoodhew.com

Made in the USA
Lexington, KY
31 March 2017